Nightmare Running...

María Baranda

Nightmare Running on a Meadow of Absolute Light

Two Poems

translated by Paul Hoover

Shearsman Books

First published in the United Kingdom in 2017 by
Shearsman Books
50 Westons Hill Drive
Emersons Green
BRISTOL
BS16 7DF

Shearsman Books Ltd Registered Office
30–31 St. James Place, Mangotsfield, Bristol BS16 9JB
(this address not for correspondence)

www.shearsman.com

ISBN 978-1-84861-543-4

ACKNOWLEDGEMENTS

'Yegua nocturna corriendo en un prado de luz absoluta,' was published by
Dirección de Literatura, UNAM / Ediciones Sin Nombre of Mexico City in
2013. UNAM also published the author's *El mar insuficiente: Poesía 1989-2009*,
in which 'Narrar' appeared.

CONTENTS

Introduction

María Baranda is one of the leading Mexican poets of the generation born in the 1960s. Her work has received Mexico's distinguished Efraín Huerta and Aguascalientes national poetry prizes, as well as Spain's Francisco de Quevedo Prize for Ibero-American Poetry. Encouraged in her youth by the great Colombian poet and writer, Álvaro Mutis, she is increasingly known for her sweeping and incisive long poems and book-length projects, such as the sequence, 'Letters to Robinson.' Of the volume, *Ficticia*, in which the Robinson poems appear, Forrest Gander writes that María Baranda "keeps honing in on one of the most expressive lyricisms in contemporary Mexican poetry." He refers also to "her complex prosody—the pitch and tempo rising in plangent cadences that break into sharp, percussive counterpoint." The sea setting of her volume *Ficticia* (2006/2010) is in perfect keeping with Baranda's verbal momentum. Despite being epic in weight and size, her poems do not patiently narrate. Their way of telling is instead a stark announcement of being similar to an invocation; for instance, in *Narrar* (2001):

> A cry that in itself
> is the size of the sea
> and lives at the center of rapture
> and with each step it yields
> to the delirium of a sponge
> that inflates in sweat and gives glory
> to the time of silent prayers
> A cry is the caiman's vigil
> the unleashed whip of an ant

For Baranda, narration is not of social relations but of the essential. Her cry is resoundingly of sea, sponge, ant, and prayer, as related in rapture. The poem's broad perspective may be influenced by the intensity and range of Vicente Huidobro's Altazor, an untranslatable word that joins "high" (*alta*) with "hawk" (*azor*):

> I love my eyes and your eyes and eyes
> Eyes with their own flash-point
> Eyes that dance to the sound of an inner music

And open like a door onto a crime
And abandon their orbits and go off like bloodstained
    comets into chance
Eyes so sharp they leave wounds that are slow to heal
And can't be closed like an envelope
                (Trans. Eliot Weinberger)

Unlike Huidobro, Baranda does not introduce the "I" of herself as author. She richly embodies the other. The speaker, we know from the Góngora epigraph, is "it." Therefore, the cry is of a universal voice, of the sky, a dolphin, and the caiman's vigil. Baranda's lyrical agency is of course significant.

Despite the richness of her verbal weave, the mention of Góngora should not suggest that Baranda is *barroco* in her poetics. In the fierce literary politics of Mexico City, strongly impacted by the dominance of men, she stands as an independent figure. She is a poet of epic vision, who views the broader tapestry of fate, in which we might recognize "an agonizing smile / in the punctual / sweetness / of the one who is drowning." That vision ranges from "the newlywed God" (an impostor) to "the sharp bite of hunger / under the yoke of a sugar mill."

The reference in 'Narrar' to a *tokonoma* leads us to the poem 'Pavilion of Nothingness' ('El pabellón de la vacuidad') by José Lezama Lima, the Cuban writer recognized as establishing the neobarroco mode of Latin American literature. A tokonoma is an alcove in traditional Japanese houses that is reserved for the display of wall-scrolls and art objects. In his poem, the tokonoma represents the imaginative power of emptiness waiting to be filled. In Baranda's work as in Lezama-Lima's, many figures compete for metaphorical control of that alcove. Characterized by layers and multiplicities, their work communicates both the provisional and necessary. The provisional act of Lezama-Lima is to cut a crevice with his fingernail in the paper wall of the tokonoma. All is made possible, from kangaroos to sapodilla ice cream, by that one marking, analogous to the pen on paper. In Baranda's poem, a "maelstrom of all the whales in the sea" is invoked. We speak of the "purely poetic," but the poetic includes the nearly empty shrine of possibility and the messy actuality of life. Baranda works toward the maximal and the simultaneous, where the motive is fate. The drama of her cadences in Spanish is not disguised by the English translation. For a more perfect knowledge of 'Narrar,' however, ask a Spanish speaker to recite the first movement: "al mar un grito / que se rompe y se repita / que se vacíe / y al tiempo de la sal." The rhythm of enunciation is remarkable, especially when Baranda herself is the speaker.

María Baranda's poetry has been translated into English, French, Lithuanian, Turkish, and Italian. Her poetry books in English are *Ficticia*, translated by Joshua Edwards (Shearsman Books, 2010) and *If We Have Lost our Oldest Tales*, translated by Lorna Shaughnessy (Arlen House, 2006).

In his preface to *If We Have Lost Our Oldest Tales*, Anthony Stanton notes her special relationship with the long poem, a poetic form which he calls "one of the great achievements of modern Western verse."[1] Stanton specifically remarks on her connection to the long poems of Saint-John Perse, Vicente Huidobro, Sor Juana Inés de la Cruz, and José Gorostiza, author of *Muerte sin fin* (Endless Death). Her proclivity for the long poem began with her first book, *El jardín de los encantamientos* (The Garden of Enchantments), published in 1989.

I selected Baranda's long poem, 'Nightmare Running on a Meadow of Absolute Light' for its force of language, dreamlike power, and connection to the poetry of Sor Juana Inés de la Cruz, whose words, taken from 'First Dream,' are embedded and scattered through sections of Baranda's poem.

Even the title of Baranda's poem, 'Nightmare Running on a Meadow of Absolute Light,' reflects the power of her subjects and themes. She strikes for the magical and the essential. The poem concludes with the intense four-page coda, 'Víbora':

> And I said viper and saw myself unscrewed, cardial and unique,
> carnivalesque and spoken, more vivid by means of the simple
> tree of language, first among the gestures of all that blood
>
> gone from my eyes toward a point of-what-other, with the root
> certainty of how-one-is-made at that time only
> when fear is inscribed among the folds of the skin.

The viper is a figure for the poet as a shifting and enfolding mage; it is also the poem, 'Nightmare Running,' with its page by page transformations. The quotations from Sor Juana, which appear in bold-face, lend an interruptive quality that is new to Baranda's work; for example:

---

[1] Galway, Ireland: 2006, p. 7.

It will have (**to climb**) to look over the night,
the first, (**trying**) to listen
their multitude (**the stars**) of wes-wes-wes
a little bit (**while**) in the half-hearted
those who await (**their lights**) and chat away
over there (**beautiful**) outside.
O those who (**without**) pray and invoke:
runners (**always**) of thorns,
time (**always**) dilated
between the (**dazzling**) needles of a lower site
enclosed (**the dark**) between spikes and barbs
below the light (**war**) green:
trees (**that with black**) liquids
between (**vapors**) or other punctuated places.
points where (**become intimate**) it sees itself
news (**the terrifying**) fall in the eye
and the eye (**shadow**) opens
to a single mouth (**fugitive**) silent.

It is also possible to read the boldface as its own postmodern lyric ("the terrifying / shadow / fugitive"). The phrase "wes-wes-wes" is an approximation of the Baranda's "oes-oes-oes," suggestive of the Spanish word "oeste" (west).

María Baranda is at her full strength as a poet and deserves to be better known by readers of English. As Mexican critic José María Espinasa wrote in support of *Ficticia*, "María Baranda is today one of our country's necessary poets."

Paul Hoover

To Tell

Its horrendous voice, not its inner sorrow
    —Góngora

A cry
just a cry
a single cry
to the open air
a cry of porpoise or dolphin
of incandescent fish by the water
a cry of the sea that breaks and repeats
that empties
and in the time of salt
says everywhere what it says that swells
that glows
a cry
a single cry
just a cry
of the blue inconceivable sky
that repeats
that advances
that grazes among the algae
the fetid rumor of the brackish
a providential cry in the voice of air
an unsustainable rhythm
in the throat
A cry that knots itself
in symphonic circles of joy
A terrible cry
that announces the first death
that stands on precarious feet
and dismantles shadows and grumbling
A cry that must choose
for between the walls the liquid deepens

The wall as a cardinal point
an agonizing smile
in the punctual
sweetness
of the one who is drowning

A cry disbanded
in a garden with thickets
a dream of blue light for the birds
A cry that in itself
is the size of the sea
and lives at the center of rapture
and with each step it yields
to the delirium of a sponge
that inflates in sweat and gives glory
to the time of silent prayers
A cry is the caiman's vigil
the unleashed whip of an ant
the fan of yes the same immaculate
air of an inhospitable grudge
that bends
The cry that smells of salt
a wild beast dry
horny
in the dusky collapse
of your herd
The cry distilled from minutes
marks the world that is world forever
in an open moment where never
passes nothing and everything dissolves
hurling itself to the bottom

Nothingness is reason falling
finally it's emptiness
its bend in the road most refreshing
when the tree
is erected in delirium

in order to sing from its purgatory
its novice illusions
almost vertigo

A cry is sleepless in its dream
faded almost hoarse it stuns itself
like a crippled animal
the cry breathes sleep inside
its eyes and evokes a sacrifice
a dark joy in a spiral of weeping

The cry moans weeps wallows
glacial polygamous decrepit
sinking into flakes and scales
into mud
the cry sleeps alone
in the hollow of useless blindfolds
its intoxicated pallor
in its cadence and fatigue
it buzzes between the glasses and the cans
the remains are still ripe
and the sweet song
of the flies to vacancy

The cry is deeply in love
and sweet together with the soft souls
Rose to call it rose
is a corrupt luxury
a brief heart
that detracts
The cry is the insistence
on misery is the sharp bite of hunger
under the yoke of a sugar mill
a fire burning
among dogs and rats
is a shadow that crosses
the fetid waters of wonder

and it's the clamor of three nights
of the sickness of women, hens, and female deer
when the gods
lose their harmony and quickly
offer their shame to the twilight

The cry is air
air that only blossoms
in the half-light of funerals
The cry is the voice of the obsequies
a wafer in the pupils
which prays "Praise be to God
without God's silent cry
infinitely bitter and dry
and the newlywed God the round impostor
who belches who vomits who repeats
fragrant at the pit and doesn't say
not to purify the skin
devour candles and beautify
blind beneath the definitive sun
lethargic in the accounting
of a glass beaded God summit
red-hot incredulous God
who doesn't ask for pardon
in the omen of dead birds."

A cry
just a cry
a single cry
it whips in lines
and looks dissolved
between the vertices of song
(sings among the captive petals
And don't forget me in the diaspora
sing sing deadly like an archangel
about about to shout his song)
The cry is erased

between the breasts that slander
sinks convenes seizes
becomes and is consumed
penetrates licks fits
in cartilage of fire
where it resides

The cry is just a number
a notch at the base of the wall
as meticulous
as a *tokonoma*
utmost swiftness of spirit
freezes the Cuban's print
bevels the aperture in the absurd
that dominates corners of the language
that exposes itself as a maelstrom
of all the whales in the sea
is an emaciated shell
adhering to the pale shadow
that crosses our sleep
The cry
is a mixture of sperm
and civil life
in living circumstances
a sign of those black fruits
where peace putrefies
streaked by oblivion
where their error is overheard
in a Parthenon of voices
and the air unfolded fornicates
voluptuously and never knows
of the children awakening
in endless tunnels
lost

The cry
roams the meadows climbs sandbanks

is hidden in the smallest grains of the sap
and splits into two branches
at the curb
of the public gardens
Its light is a wandering stage
where the bodies drink
unchangeable as
the dried blood of vultures
The cry becomes stained, expands
to a canvas painted in bleach
and to moist fish markets in the cracks
that drip their thirst in cathedrals
It calls between shingles and gutters
for the white popcorn of mercy
It doesn't exist
in the vaults that invoke
either groans or excrement
they pour out their prayer to beauty

The cry looks and turns nutritious
among the filaments
subtleties of stalagmites
Its opacity contains and glorifies
the scars of crazy widows
the plagues of corrupted young women
At the center it's gripped at the edge
A luminous crust between the slabs
At night the bodies whip it
they lick it like a cat at the touch
in its delirium In its crevices
the world opens in a color in passage
it flaps its wings in sheets of salt in its integrity
and among the porticos
it feels its furtive gifts
of the filthiest birds in the land
The cry of a flowing spring that overcomes time
soothing of the wrong man

As an insect
lands on the leavening
and gives voice to the rhizome of God
between the lips "die
with bags under your eyes by the name
where quicklime levies a tax
on your dead children"
The cry is only a cry
of silky smoothness where a theologian
lives morbidly in dirty rags in small rooms
Slowly it's known in the cloudy discharge
at random in broken windows
The cry is the pigment of an incantation
between the orchards and the fruit
of fervent prayer
Drop by drop it sings limitless
in a pit of sky-blue ineptitude
where it drinks the blood by sips
and swigs and names the food
of the executioner
Its bitterness is slow
with the dryness of a sponge
lifeless and scratchy
its devotion like a fever
(To Dimas it tasted like salt
in his bleeding
In Barabbas it was only a fruit
a swordfish in the balance
on the cross exhausted)

Humble and persistent the cry
it is always the acid that saturates us
in agony a single weeping that spills
in the slow endless afternoons of suicide

A cry
exceeds climbs sweats

when God tells us numbly
there are no nails no rituals
in the recurring tumors of the righteous
The sun burns your tongue microscopic
in the crack that robs us
dropwise prim and proper

There is a thirst that refreshes us in clouds
In the briefest cottons
of urgent slowness
There is a threadbare tethering
in the stillness of a tree
or in the piles of stones that wall us in
the blood in the waste land
if the cry grows in variety
profuse by the fire
fragrant crazed
from being the deaf hollows
that nest in men

The cry
opens its strength with a wedge
and falls silent where light doesn't sing
where silence
is an openness of the spirit
Its spirit in self-controlled scales
is a source
symphonic in color
and the vertigo that rises in the corner
in which I am at the precipice
in the millimetric skimming
of the page

This is what I am and what I cry
that I am not boneless
given to babbling
a smooth speech

that which my blood speaks one before
one after the world and for the eyes
a warm animal that centers me
Wolves hyenas coyotes in my
heart inside the sumptuous
porphyry of blood
they gasp and they feed
on the warm flesh
that hastens the blood in me

Flesh of a cry I am
in proletarian forests
in indigent caves
where the vultures
in my voice defecate
centuries into the future
Meat asleep a cry
waiting on the shore
a convenient body
yellowed and rotten
so that it burns
so that it is
still
so that yet

A cry
just a cry
a single cry measures
a metropolis
and refers
to the apostolic light that awaits
where never
nor no one
nor either

So that it speaks
so that it hears

its galaxy of dirty white stains
its sweet germination of clots and appendices
its drunkenness and such ecstatic weeping
that hosts and increases
its thirst on which it agonizes
and slows down in the arrogant
capital of merged lines
banished
Lightning by day
is the fury of the cry
if it goes clumsily jogging
on the ledge if confused
fragrant and so very semantic
where for you for me for everyone
trembling abdicates
its tin-plated trot
its rhythmic tension in every muscle
is a passing with no one on the horizon
riding as if nothing
ever departed or faded
for centuries unclear
for the fetal prairie of the deceased
where time nests among vipers
and agonized men redeem
the muffled hum of dreams
in the dream of being silent
its lying silence centuries of death

To cry or not to cry is the question
The stone that scarifies
and arises in only a face
in onyx borax flint
the triangular stone of an episcopal
silicate where the air crackles
the world of a slingshot
contained
in ulcers of shadows

The stone from the ruins that assays itself
where there once was a cry or outbreak
in the instant in which it envisions
the blinking blue of the disasters:
that time when we lost
the rage of children unburied
(The stone the cry the outbreak
the hour in which the night
is twice
brief)

At last the secular water reached me
it looked at me face to face with the stones
of a pool architectural and empty
where the cry lives in its
eager bloodless
anonymous monastery
its century of sinister
meetings
red-hot
stopped between my lips

To the fire suspended in air
the sentry song
invites cries
to a pile of sticks where silently the birds
peck twice at a corpse
a soul with so many flies discoursing
among its orifices
making love
wound to wound

The cry in me is power and pride
if I touch it with my voice
unnoticed in the tumult
an ash tree in the air a ceiba
flanking the cemeteries

when the dense grass spreads over
their corpses
in the offices of my skin
The circular cry is a eulogy
disobedient
scattered snow briefly
bridal "all her beauty"
a name almost a wound
"and nevertheless we had to kill her"
referred to on the scaffold
where such a white
"look at the veil and the gown"
the firmament of the sheet
in her monthly bleeding
is hidden in the sum of its whiteness

Ceremonial
the cry is just a cry
and nothing more as I listen
astonished to die in its silence

Nobody despises its vertigo
of a slave and functionary
accompanied by ignorance
or remorse
in amazement
to be dead to be said
translucent in the shroud
of smoke of the perjuries of water
sipped thus very small
the cry in ignorance proclaims itself
a knotted thread
an astrological body vertiginous
a thread a heart a penumbra
to say that it goes that it burns deeply
that among your children it stretches out the rope
it always hides or the crossbow

that hurls its announcements
from one side to another in the eyes
Its language is heard in a rustling
and it sinks in a temple of love
is pierced spits up
a gob
like a soft *tin tin*
becoming the largest
among the small
that inwardly
they transmute its memory
and obscure
the most confusing shadow
the least by way of the slightest
in a crack where the cries
are the ravenous joy
of optimum acquiescence

A cry is entangled in marrow
and in veins still growing green it settles
along with the beat of my will
assumed snorting the immune air
cloudy loudmouth of appetite
Milestones of salt and foam
iridescent
rave and in docile waves they decode
scrupulously its tardiness

Its tardiness from being a single bone
of the skeleton
a clamor crammed with images
that denies
its first time
held back
from entering this world for the first time

The cry is a burning instant
swollen
in the ruckus written in lightning
it cradles that which devours it
steams in the mists and sustains
the merciful warmth of being alive

The cry appears transposes suffocates
condemning the embrace of lucidity
in blind women
The cry is frozen if you lift it
in that paradise where it scrutinizes
its condolences of carnivorous rain
To the water that rises absorbed
within itself
drop by drop
it invades limits makes expensive
the voice doesn't move toward another shore
Its nearness dissolves us
leaves us stunned and sickly
just scraping by our souls in our laps
exhausted in fiber and thread
Languid the leanness in corpses
it switches on at the neck
dreaming by means of lugubrious salt
the latest iterations of the one who dies

Suffocation of my suffocation
in clouds of smoke
real as green gold
that arrives and falls to pieces
in diaphanous wisps where it burned
my sad territory of mercenary shadows
the cry in its place of honor
testified to the dust
and the melancholy enclosures
of mistletoe that purifies

that doesn't measure up
that makes my chess moves
and turns and turns
like the mad queen
that inhabits me
(it was my mother her pallor
of a handmaid of the sky) gray
in the fervor
gray if balanced
and drips
prisoner of her own arguments
(at fifteen
the cry in packs
traveled through my womb)

In its modesty and its ablution
in love with little girls
the cry runs according to the laws
that keep carrion tidy
and discredits it
quietly
in the writing

The cry is the mouth of absence
a moaning hole where it so happens
the world's procedures are hardened
(the being without being that covers us
and matures us
in the laps of assassins)
The cry is the pit of life
the pubis shaved of its scapulars
The cry is the end that unfolds
in the climax that anoints families

At its brink the old resist the abyss
for its angle of light is extended
in the wick

Lichens illustrate them
impetuous discreet accomplices
on a battlefield

In March it coincides with a spore
in May it's the hair gel of intrigue
in July it's only a fit of rage
a lunar prodigal in August
Its cadences are lewd in months
Its name contains the zodiac
In public squares its succinct thicket
murmurs a circle of herbs for fever
Only a moment from its gesture to touching
scrawny the cries are disheveled
they roar among the jump ropes
In bulbs they iridesce us
our brief beating in prayers
Cries to the death
are the image of God close to the earth
In the children of night they burn

A cry is seeing up close
and demarcating the boundaries
of drowning among the pelicans
in fine dreams of gannets
In its stems the Eucharist shines
knowing the curves of Caravaggio
In the shining sun In the canvas
they implore the waters renewed
in the ink almost loving
almost
true

Horns are blown
over nothing over all they rave
in engravings of the redeemed saints
(Here someone bleeds for the cry

a lip a black incision
outside by the wall)

If I cry leafy
the birds are entrusted
accentuating deeply
the limbo of frost
the ferment in my blood
for the world If I am quiet
my tongue is grafted
eventful and surges
denigrating
darker and darker inside me
A cry opens and finds its place
in order to love death
the beautiful inexhaustible
the single death that stretches
and always
when I write
with my mouth
it is my companion

Agamic in liturgical night
the dust raised by a letter
has no end does not ignore
the passages that hide
the courtyard of the blood
the laps of blind mothers
haunt its furious fading
blow by blow in what is rooted
in the flesh of the beholder
and does not go silent
artisan stormy
and so fruitful

Its tongue conjectures in silence
and in the soft flowering that guards it

obscene it wanders the atrophied limb
of the winged unsatisfied thought
brutal
as the knife it raises

The cry is split in two by the thorn
(The grapevine where it wiped
sublime the heart
one Nemeroso extended
to heaven in his fall to the field
on behalf of Salicio)
running through the story
awakening
together with green peaks
Nothing remains of it
unprotected by any sacrament
the life that it didn't love
the solitary death that punches holes
in your pages flying to the vanquished
It has no spores
in its incompleteness
the air drags it
like water
to another owner
never to places
that possess mirrors
No shape remains
of its shape nothing remains
We know by
the dream that resounded
golden and shivering
everything so yes
spherical unbounded
with difficulty
for example

In loyal tastes of its own flesh
the cry exudes in saltpeter
congenial opening out it falls
purifying itself
in garments of cloth pustules
that glorify

Its no-place
is the password to vacancy
that grows empty
only in it
in a breath of love
you move out
already they exhale it

The cry is just a woolen weave
of faces in scrolls
flying in misery
at the top of the world
limitless

And on behalf of the world
if only the world
poured itself out
and was a single fold
in the golden foul-mouthed thirst
of life
then
avid and scattered and vigilant
perhaps
it will happen
in an amen without a mass celebrated
oxidizing in a *snip snip*
the song and the shroud
if certain to be unborn
in its innocence to be
what pulls off its petals

addict to whom
all was equal
the branch and dust
of the dust of the earth
If a voice in a voice is broken
too much
lyric arborescence in pop lyric
amber that hides forever
a translucent rock
of honey for the throat
If arriving in pain
so that
you appeared to be dying among the letters
scattered
and since
without hope
if so much alone

A cry
just a cry
a single cry
of everything to all
flows and conjectures
in the finest bursts saying
they are going to love you
only you
you procreate with him
the fleeting shadow
and the ash
there
the breeze at the bottom
of humiliation

The cry breathes
and rubs
the fragments
of you of me

why if where
it doesn't go it doesn't advance
never says
here!
in the purple salt
dripping
your last drop
always
and for the world

To the sea to the sky to the river
just a cry
a cry

Nightmare Running
on a Meadow
of Absolute Light

for Sofia and Jimena

The world enlightened and I awaken

Sor Juana Inés de la Cruz

And nevertheless, here

almost

unsuspected, tired of seeing the voices

stripped from the land

—another earth, other lips of another cutting—

the modesty

of the flowers that torment, how much

brightness looms

at the edge of everything

and therefore

what's not known.

And I,

why didn't I know

of me?

Otherworldly, delirious,

unapproachable

at a point

pertaining to and named

pendulum

in the eye

uncorked: covered in dust: placed

removed

and discarded.

It burns and declines

alone,

infinitely alone,

pounded, dismembered, broken

despised and deflated

it arises

in the shadows,

nightmare

running

on a meadow of absolute

light

...and when I ask myself

who could be persuaded

seeing that sonorous sky,

the open breach in the wall,

the movement in its measure

and the field in a fabric of herbs

sustained in its membranes,

alone, so alone, exhaling

a new punctuation, a long

cry in the aggravated night,

forced to see

a glimmer of what was,

telling yourself the same:

bad, worse, terrible,

and I think about this disproportion

of thought,

in the astonishment before a pause,

a compass stopped

on a non-existent phone or on a CD

timorous and solicitous, a *now*

in its intent to be flame

between even darker lips

when the fish,

you said, were twice

speechless

always in the cavern

where the sun opens

disobediently

a defense

against the darkness

or a simple opaque

form

that you saw among atoms

and molecules,

dreamed?

You briefly switch on a galaxy and touch your childhood sea. The world is a dark road where night is the voice of what you say. At the sound of water you think of celestial birds, clouds, and a bit of sun in a story that begins without words.

....because I look far away

fallen to the bottom, caught in the mud,

hidden in slow, solitary thickness,

because I say *fire*

and it rushes from my mouth

in flames,

because I name you now

as then

and the birds are more fragile and the clouds

no longer exist,

because I see you on the path of high stone

that imagines high meadows, diverse,

and the inhospitable matter

where articles

in the same reflection

that walks and talks and evaporates

and because everything is a page of hunger

where you reconcile the impossible

with only the single sun in syllables of the Advent,

because the night,

this night,

night vitreous and tiny

the most furious and insistent

which oxidizes itself as lightning

with this high form

has a putrid empire

with its eyes wide open, its field

of aromas in cages

its cry like a mean mule

that never forgets

—no—

and that it is there together with us

in order to die a little

from time to time and with the sleep

that is night,

that night

unique and pyramidal,

and completely yours.

The dogs of night break out of their dreams together. They lose their eyes. You clarify reality with the laughter of the waters. Then the world goes missing to ride on a single wave like a lament in the burning arousal of cholera.

…and when I hear of the style

in which the wind howls over those old

flowery faces of clay, I think

of what this city reveals

and hastily burns

in my hands,

in that same history

corrupted,

where I gulp it down blindly

in dark streets of ink and iron

traced in the dust

that roars alone,

where I see it plainly

and I am soon ready

to take slow sips

among the rats

and garbage dumps

centuries ago where you sang

and I feel it, her crush

on you

in my throat

like a cry

and stings

in its orphanhood of mud

and presents itself and me

dislocated

while the dogs

lick saltpeter

from the dead walls

and roll tinplate cans

kicked by the laughter

of children

Its rattle brings up in me

a flower of rapid water

in their drains

and leaves me

beneath scabby heaven

listening to its gravel

of *vegetative color*,

its separate arms

extending

a dry cry, slow

in the repentance

on fire.

Toc-toc-toc, change your name. You appear like a woodpecker in the evening. Nothing now remains. Outside, rocks growl in the jaws of the fog. You'd like to be an alphabet that spells the flight of the insect, a disappointment of the relentless sun, with the high force of your instinct splitting to pieces.

Light blindly, light

uncertain, light of mud,

light undulation of time

in the uproar of my fronds.

Light

of water, light incomplete,

light morally unfolded

uprooted pleading with your own

lips

don't let me

fall

into the heavens I don't know

stars to me

nearby

and deep in the dream

of the dream

that moans me and establishes what only I recognize.

It talks of clouds.

It precedes.

It shakes

and unveils.

It cries out to its mother,

icy wind

beneath the grass.

It's refractory.

In the shadows

it refrains

and consecrates.

Grouped

in their own language: it ceases.

And loves.

...Pyramidal, terrible, of the land

We could have been the abyss:

the conclusion that this something that fell off soon,

but only saw the spectacles

of a new era: the scribbled sigh

of someone who cried "homeland," the hand

signaled in the mercury that knew the memory

of mutant legal history, the enmity

that clamored "I am, I am" and abstracted itself

ad nauseam in the apotheosis of an entire paradise.

Your cry wheels in the abyss. You invoke invisible loves, broken caves where your blood can navigate the divinations of the slopes.

... Pyramidal, terrible, of the land

We could. We could have been different

as if we improvised a face

in the bluest lens, even more

than the story of a plastic and future Aegean.

Together we pass now by the pond of thought

and its disagreements, where the truth

is only this breathed air, this dry laughter, and soon,

in a previous sentence, in an idea that we defend

as if beyond a bright hope of the dead

intolerably ours. And we could say: this is the site,

and someone could pass very close and remember

how love was under the green veins of dread,

or simply name to another the course of the day,

in order later to fold the little paper slips of sweets

and save them.

There is a flame that is your shadow. It burns in the swell of the impossible while the others light only half of their lives.

...Pyramidal, terrible, of the land

All in a demonstration of time,

in a shrine that responds to the distance,

to an imaginary place as if it were only a form,

even the name that soon remembers

the dinners filled with voices,

the voices of the son

that are disguised and transmuted and awkwardly

encounter the routine of being.

You take each sip of the rain's madness and you slip past the bridges pierced by the howls of wolves. You open your legs. There is no steppe that does not burn with your song of mud and fire, with the heat of your voice in its prayers.

...Pyramidal, terrible, of the land

All the while death outlines

a ritual fasting as if it were possible

to keep oblivion speedily,

not to have been nor ever part

of a fixed fear, fear of the last gasp

and being crossed out, fear that passes and returns

to pass squeaking and biting, sunken and concave,

blistering and plaintive.

Holes of mud. The plain that fills a solitude the size of your night. The first night. The one offering sleep fermented in scars. You decide to chisel your death onto another surface.

…here there are no cows that can **climb**

the streets, nor the **terrible**

precaution of birds

biting the trunk of days.

Here amulets languish in silence

and silence breaks into particles so small

they can hear the cry, the true cry,

that in a separate **shadow**

standing speaks

with its legs.

Here they crack

the **vain** bulbs of night

that germinate and plunge

in the moisture of

a fraction of soil

where the voice is heard

trying

to break and enter with its tongue

Calculations, quills, Cathars, monarchs that pronounced fine gargoyles in your throat. You speak moist vapors and in the fire sermon the poplars burn at the sound of their voices.

...it would have a *(pyramidal)* curve and back

all of a (*terrible*) surface.

the part (*of the land*) in front

that shows us (*born*) the painful step

of a feline (*shadow*). It would have

to procure (*for heaven*) the edges

the mouths that (*directed*), recover

moisture (*in vain*) to the bark

the rest of an (*obelisk*) prairie of rice

that splendid (*tip*) its downfall

before the eyes of a (*proud*) open flower. It would have.

Shadows that cock your head like erect and brutal fish among the pages of a stubborn astronomy. There is no oblivion. Everything is the new alien and boisterous way of those who don't know to cry the harsh blood that was lost in their dreams.

It will have (**to climb**) to look over the night,

the first, (**trying**) to listen

their multitude (**the stars**) of wes-wes-wes

a little bit (**while**) in the half-hearted

those who await (**their lights**) and chat away

over there (**beautiful**) outside.

O those who (**without**) pray and invoke:

runners (**always**) of thorns,

time (**always**) dilated

between the (**dazzling**) needles of a lower site

enclosed (**the dark**) between spikes and barbs

below the light (**war**) green:

trees (**that with black**) liquids

between (**vapors**) or other punctuated places.

points where (**become intimate**) it sees itself

news (**the terrifying**) fall in the eye

and the eye (**shadow**) opens

to a single mouth (**fugitive**) silent.

Indignities in the rain. Star clusters that name God among your bones. They attack your armies of shadows from Alpha Centauri until the new galaxies are inscribed on your eyelids. Your eyelids: stone suns that declined his light for a mere rumor from another universe.

...to arrive at the form, **the stars**, in slow division

to write once again and another **hoping**

when at bottom we could speak silt

and **climb**

the richness of the pen (**lofty**), the language

of another saturation

of the **tip** and their fate in the mud.

And in the end, obelisks, among those

wastes of birds

vain and crude,

we could return to say: as if

then **of** what flowed out

it was perhaps a glyph

or a crack that **directed**

the air and the air its fullness

in heaven. What is formed

in the form of **shadow born**

of the earth and leaves us (leaves you)

terrible,

returning us (returning you)

slowly

pyramidal towards others

so terrified and alone.

Broken conversations. Fragments. You look for that way of writing among scorpions. You lick a little flour between your palms. You observe the turn of the spinning top of your language. You are more alone always, from the dawn of your dream to the large glass of your days.

...and as it would have left the form,

pyramidal, clumsy and slow, **terrible**

one against the other

in order to find

on the earth an exit

simpler and more resistant, something

that included **birth**,

not only the word **shadow**

but make it a perfect

unique and proliferating circle

that, at the same moment, **the sky**

seeks to turn

as if it were a flash

that **directed** other metaphors,

a place

of vain sounds in the embankment,

obelisks of ideas

or a space at each turn

of the year that proclaimed

the **point** most perfect,

the magma inside

the **loftiest** part, foremost

and fecund, where

to climb, only to climb,

was not to know

that sleep was there

like a dry branch

aspiring to be

a false mask

in the disfiguration

of all **the stars**.

From there the photos, papers,

the writing desk on one's shoulders

in the eye of the eye of the snake.

Your ideas fall into the abyss of pencils while the early morning stretches to give you a dream. Only one, as the fresh sweetness of your blood arises. Reflections that flash in the Milky Way, sad explanations for sad situations.

Light

possible, light launched

small

in the line that frightens

in the hinge of my pen,

interior,

do not

permit

suspicion

to follow

from body to body

or the designs of ink

in yearning and defeat

invisible fragments in the owl's cage

and far

from me

all ties

nothing disturbs what the emptiness

doesn't give.

Vast

in number

wounded and overheated

it frightens the little ones

robs nymphs, harms

hunger.

It crosses the threshold

of its lair

Almost dragging on,

almost vile

and true.

It consecrates abandonment

to establish

its new home,

internal and indissoluble.

It thrives.

...and any and all have been

returned, like a blessing to the verb

and nevertheless

muddy vipers hang

on hooks, smooth

atmospheres of salt,

residues on the lips

of so many poor,

five children of nickel

carved into my skull,

summers foaming in speech

and fear of the belt

in the estimate of what

distant mothers, inmates

who reverberate offended

in the darkest lime,

five mirrors tight

in the ice of cold

hopelessness and the shutters

in the poplar tree, chalice to the vertigo

of our languages,

more beautiful than the light

of an empty box,

all of it returns

and comes into agreement

and phrases its own

fragility,

perceives itself

as a life of nothing

as if someone moaned

in alcohol something

that was not ours

and suddenly returned

and thought

not being / not having

in its own passage

and defeat and nevertheless,

like a blessing to the verb,

now.

The inscrutable proliferates. Confusion reddens the body and their approaches to the shore of an implausible papyrus where everything is black and red and very deep and confines the night in the sorrow of deterioration.

...shoring up the form and coming near,

enclosing the face and drawing its shadow,

speak the body like an asylum

that only protects and always strikes

straight to the way, noisy and possible,

of the new surface.

There is no density

if the unquiet

distance

is what it represents.

There was a mirror, its share

of memory,

the perfect size,

recurring time,

the harvest where the cry stifled

all that is possible.

And then the hand

and its insult transformed,

its music

and the second shadow of the fog.

Fresh words are your fate, the instrument of a time in decline which means an era and its frightening syllabification. That which defines. That which you love.

...corridors of those who capitulate,

body next to body

in a closed cube,

cube that means

house and *promise*,

a broken heaven

and the hard, hollow face

of your childhood days.

Pins that touch and

abrade the ground,

on a night broken

and distant, from which you still

cannot awaken,

because the world

sustains you

impending and accidental.

Threads that hang

from your tongue,

the desperate

corners of an open mourning

dilating in the simple,

and in what is not,

it never occurred

and will not branch off,

Thousands of wings in

thousands of avenues made

available to no one,

at a single dead and atrocious point.

As the point you love.

Which is chopped off

by a voice

without memory and sense,

lost in your unique name,

without a name,

in the empty

rooms.

In what century

are you named?

Everything is sinking into its own downfall, in the repairing of an apocryphal thought. You say the stone and verify the principle of this world. You run to the bottom of the sky and it accidentally drops from your mouth. The balance is always a rift that opens in your dreams.

...and still I return to you

before the sun puts to sleep

the toughest birds on Earth,

you don't say where

to strike, you wake up

among flowers

that receive your wounds,

don't count when

you grieve on a green dawn

you noisily defied

if at the murmuring margin,

I remain you, change

in the breast of March

while the sun paints

its memory in crude blue,

you never say

if the vertigo, in its obsession,

creates you

—irrigates you—

time being alone,

you who live undefeated

under the impetus

of proliferating truth,

you in your first nudity,

abandon the sun to proclaim the sun,

the wandering clarity of blood,

and that we

remain blind to you,

and illuminated in the distance

that love

procures.

Everything burns while you burn the heart of the wind as if it were the skin of a viper. Wake up! In your voice, the world is just beginning.

Víbora

i

And I said *viper* and saw myself unscrewed, cardial and unique,
carnivalesque and spoken, more vivid by means of the simple tree of
language, first among the gestures of all that blood

gone from my eyes toward a point of-what-other, with the root
certainty of how-one-is-made at that time only
when fear is inscribed among the folds of the skin.

And then, my flesh fixed in ink, congealed, I imagined
what I am, in that reality among the weeds
conceived in too much shade, too much hunger

hopelessly seeking the cry, my lips still pressed together
where it repeats and is exalted, wraps itself in yes,
always changing in nature in order to say: I am language.

I was language on another cracked scale and sweet
to place in the mouth, a pleasure of speech that shines:
I said *viper* and it was ample, opulent, a certain female bird

naked before heaven, fog turned into lips and said: again
to say *girl* in the animal's shadow, in the dark space
in that cry written where it's read in fullness: *poem.*

ii

Blood in the vena cava. It can't endure its losses.
Venous blood in the anterior, speeding in droves
in that swallowing of one and another by an uncertain word...

or in that soft part where you drink the abandonment
of an idea that contains all of us, delays and
subjugates us before the silence of an indivisible figure:

the verb, the pure verb. The heart is quenched, defeats
maternal dreams beneath the crystalline fangs
like a dark and humid sun full of nothing and time. Time

that uncoagulates, spreading far beyond those wastelands, uninhabited
and muddled in the head. They drink, their lips
avid for other numbers, decantings, prophecies in water:

like a dense cloud you were created, baroque and resurgent,
your name fallen in the gallop of what's easier like insistence,
the repentance corrupted in your syntax. The ribs

generate gender and distance, are part of another idiom, threshold
of accents and syllables where this other innate anger arises
that shines a new fornication between your pages.

iii

Poem of the world until it becomes unique, I survive
below the language in time, bulging and successful
together with achievements where, when mixed now

and if progress is made on mothers, faithless mothers
who speak in whispers and saliva, everything's more alive
between the limbs of a violated idea.

Distances masked by mossy gold, split
timber, the locks of so many dry heavens
clinging to that cloudy and written skin.

Until what you see is heard as a howl
(take it out) almost in the far (quickly), almost
desired (say it!) like a radiating happiness?

Whatever is not is only a breath in synthesis,
profane and spoken, thought in ether for a dead frog,
as if it were a plaster statue adjacent to such sites

and where everything is purified in the hollow consolation
of always between your segments of shadow being an animal
besieged by another animal here in the fear of my mouth.

iv

Suck me slowly, interlock your syllables and sing.
Sing me. Be my circle and abandonment. Idea.
Flash of the sun in my head. Golden in me,

focused and always true. Mythical gorgon,
sculpt your forked tongue along my curves
and enthrone all that's known that loves.

It spreads the love in your breath. It weeps.
Let me write without fear or panic,
that I am pulled beyond the longest branch

and listen to your first syntax, your dream
so amorous of a bullet interred in the mountain,
inflame me in the wind playing in my name

until you make me so pregnant, like a vast
and round idea, one that covers only me
and denounce the light already separated from the sphere.

Then I say: how much of the same blood
in my body, how great the mystery that breathes
in layers and layers of words: I write.

v

There are old children already touched by other vertigos.
Angels without mirrors, nobodies who seek the misery
of a song, the hunger for an unnecessary theory.

Nothing serves, all is known to die between the avid lines
of a first branching :::
I keep an ancestral child in my bed. She bites me.

Filaments between her eyes where in a gesture an invisible
river breathes. Only one. One like a slow whisper
that poisons. Now, its tongue cries for new paradises.

Extremes of a world where the dogs lose
their bone of night. It was night when we heard
the whispers of deaf men in the corridors.

Still, there is no poem. Everything's being placed on the bricks
among the nails of the dead. Songs next to the stone,
the button of fire of an authentic mex-mex. And that's it.

Everything pleases the anonymous palate. And there are no endings.
Only a breeze like a herald of the open mother, mother CD
mother poem, sexual novice, exiled viper, mine:

vi

Kill her, milk her, take out all the juice.
Don't let her slither into consciousness.
Suck her wind's light, drain it. Call her adverb,

verb, truncated syntax, ancient alphabet: foul-mouthed.
Lose it at the edge of her figure. Stop her.
Tell her there is no sap, nor juice, nor letter.

A cavern is her language, an open container.
Her thirst is the land. Her absence. Her heart is shadow,
shell, suture of the dry land. She has no ears,

but she listens, listens under the smooth stones
hidden next to a sexless pubis. Slit with neither hope
nor daughters, limb of moist gestures, the viper

is thought, hardened reason, hollow of a god
dark and bitter, fallible and porous, smooth talker,
mound on the flatland, father, father, I said *father*

I came to tell you what mother told me to tell you
then, everything is spoken when time falters,
it whistles in its drumroll and lodges in its throat.

The Translator

Paul Hoover is the author of the poetry volumes *Desolation: Souvenir* (2012), *Sonnet 56* (2009), *Edge and Fold* (2006) and *Poems in Spanish* (2005), which was nominated for a Bay Area Book Award. He is editor of *Postmodern American Poetry: A Norton Anthology* (1994), a second edition of which appeared in 2013, and co-editor of the literary magazine, *New American Writing*. He teaches Creative Writing at San Francisco State University.

Lightning Source UK Ltd.
Milton Keynes UK
UKOW03f2333210417
299618UK00002B/465/P